GRACENOMICS
UNLEASH THE POWER OF SECOND CHANCE LIVING

PARTICIPANT GUIDE
4 DVD SESSIONS WITH MIKE FOSTER

TABLE OF CONTENTS

ACKNOWLEDGEMENTS

INTRODUCTION

16 SESSION 1: GRACE MATTERS

26 SESSION 2: GRACENOMICS FOR YOU

36 SESSION 3: GRACENOMICS FOR OTHERS

46 SESSION 4: GRACENOMICS AT WORK

56 NEXT STEPS

©2010 Mike Foster/People of the Second Chance
PO Box 513
Corona, CA 92878
www.POTSC.com
CONTACT@POTSC.com
ALL RIGHTS RESERVED.
No part of this publication may be reproduced, stored in a retrieval system, or transmitted in any form or by any means—for example, electronic, photocopy, recording—without the prior written permission of the publisher. The only exception is brief quotations in printed reviews.
Cover design and book layout by PlainJoe Studios. www.plainjoe.net
Author photograph by Trevor Hoehne.
In certain cases, the names have been changed in order to protect the privacy of the individuals mentioned in this book.
Printed in the United States of America
Visit www.POTSC.com
10 9 8 7 6 5 4 3 2 1

ACKNOWLEDGEMENTS

Thank you to Patricia Dewit, Sarah Cunningham, Becca Carroll and PlainJoe Studios, Nick Jones and Dave Schwarz at Prolifik Films, Ashley Smith and Kristen Foster for bringing your talents and efforts to this project.

Thanks to Bill Townsend, Kevin Small, Steve Graves, Jud Wilhite and Brian Johnson for your constant support and guidance.

To the incredible team at People of the Second Chance who work so diligently to unleash radical grace on a daily basis.

To the thousands of men and women who have made second chance living their chosen lifestyle. You are the movement.

06 GRACENOMICS

WELCOME

You know how some guys are obsessed with talking motorcycles? Or hunting? Or that one buzzer-beater play they were a part of back in 1983? It may seem crazy, but the thing that gets me fired up at that level these days is grace.

Seriously.

It doesn't matter what topic is up for grabs. It could be a new must-see movie, some political drama, or a new item on the lunch menu, it all somehow gets me thinking and talking about grace.

And it works the other way too. If you have a redemptive story about someone finding a second chance in life? You have me at hello. I'm putty in your hands.

Grace has become my "life message" and I have dedicated everything I have to proclaiming its necessity in our world.

As you can imagine, I have witnessed grace change up all kinds of people....including myself. I've watched grace heal broken marriages, bring hope to people at the end of their rope and bust through a teenager's self-hatred. Without exception, grace is the fuel that drives every comeback story I know.

And yet as transforming as grace is, it tends to be scarce. Even though we so desperately need and want it, there's often very little of it to go around. And that kills me. My spirit demands to know why we would ever let an idea this powerful go in short supply?

This is why I wrote the book *Gracenomics: Unleash The Power of Second Chance Living* and co-founded People of the Second Chance. Because I believe something has to change.

This need for change began to take root in me several years back as I met with a friend in a Starbucks. He had just gone through a massive failure in life. He had been involved in an inappropriate relationship, lost his job, his marriage fell apart and close friends weren't so close anymore.

He was a walking shell of a man and the weight of condemnation and failure was crushing him. It was clear that grace was basically extinct in his world.

Towards the end of our time together at the coffee shop, my friend asked, "Do you think God could ever use me again?"

He sincerely wasn't sure.

The fact that this question even existed immediately broke my heart. But it also woke me up to notice how messed up our thinking is when it comes to grace.

This is when I realized that we, people of faith, need to rethink grace. To rethink who grace belongs to and who gets to decide who does or doesn't qualify to receive it. And to rethink our role in it.

Imagine what could happen to the quantity of grace in the world if every single one of us determined to get a little bit better at giving grace. If we decided to do the impossible and forgive? If we finally let that one person we've been grudging against off the hook? If we—and maybe here's the real shocker—decided to show ourselves a little mercy?

What if a tribe of people rose up and reclaimed real grace, big grace, scandalously generous grace on behalf of the faith?

That's the point of the pages to come. To set the stage to think differently. To recalibrate our views on grace. To invite the world to it's second chance.

It is time for us to unleash second chance living.

Mike Foster
Author of Gracenomics and Co-founder
of People of the Second Chance.

HOST AND LEADER TIPS

First off, thank you for your willingness to take the initiative to begin this discussion with your friends, co-workers or family.

Small groups are ideal places to have healthy discussions about grace because grace is best learned when it can be experienced and shared with others.

As follows, we believe you are about to invite others into more than just some great discussions. For many of you, your groups will open the door for grace to change people's lives.

Here are few things to do and consider:

1. Be prepared. Review the material and watch the DVD session before everybody else. Don't try to wing it. You will get out of the group what you put into it.

2. Know your group. It is always a good idea to personally contact those who are in your group and touch base with an email or phone call letting them know you are glad they are participating.

3. Have fun. One of the best ways to draw out interaction and great conversations is to set the stage for fun. Food, drinks and some background music may really help people feel relaxed.

4. Design it for your group. The participant guide and DVD are tools to help you. But please don't feel limited by them. Put your own spin, creativity and personal expression into the content.

5. Get ready. Have the DVD ready to play and have some extra pens or pencils available for others.

6. Don't do all the talking. Again, this is a conversation so as the leader it is your job to facilitate discussion. Be a good listener.

7. Give grace. Not everyone will agree with everything that is said in the group. If you have differences in opinion, show love and respect to each other. Create a safe space to talk about hard and messy things.

8. Visit the People of the Second Chance website for other tools, ideas and content that could add to the group experience. www.POTSC.com

We would love to hear what is happening in your group. Feel free to post things online or send us an email to share your insights, celebrations or stories.

Email: Contact@POTSC.com
Twitter: @POTSC
Hashtag: #potsc
Facebook: www.Facebook.com/potsc
Website: www.POTSC.com

WHAT MATERIALS ARE NEEDED?

1. Every person attending the group should have a copy of their own participant guide.

2. The group leader should have one copy of the Gracenomics DVD.

3. Every individual should have a pen or pencil in order to write in the book.

4. It is recommended that each group member have a copy of *Gracenomics: Unleash The Power of Second Chance Living*. Group discounts are available at www.POTSC.com

INTRODUCTION

Every second a seeker can start over, for his life's mistakes are initial drafts and not the final version. --Sri Chinmoy

Keep open house; be generous with your lives. By opening up to others, you'll prompt people to open up with God, this generous Father in heaven. -- Matthew 5:16

Opportunities for grace show up in every part of our day.

Think about it.

A clueless driver cuts you off on your way to work.

A critical spouse pushes the exact right buttons.

A best friend mouths off about something that was supposed to be confidential.

A rude customer belittles your job skills.

A teen oozes entitlement and arrogance.

All of us could list several occasions in a day where grace is desperately needed. The opportunity to extend a second chance is always in front of us.

These four sessions are designed to help us identify and tune into these often overlooked areas where there is ripe opportunity to extend compassion, forgiveness and understanding.

Will all your questions about the deep implications of grace be answered when this is over? Probably not.

Will you be a grace-giving champion after you've gone through these 4 sessions? The answer to that doesn't lie with us. The *Gracenomics* materials are designed to start the dialogue and provide a beginning framework for transformational life change. What you do with the ideas—the extent to which you determine to live them out—is entirely up to you.

But we will promise you this: if you open yourself up to these teachings, you will approach conflict, disappointment, forgiveness, crisis, struggles and your relationships differently.

And it is our hope that once you taste big grace, you'll be hooked. And you'll never be able to go back to condemnation and judgment again.

We hope this will be the first day in a lifetime of second chances to come.

SESSION ONE: GRACE MATTERS

SUMMARY

Man is born broken. He lives by mending. The grace of God is glue. --Eugene O'Neill

I do not at all understand the mystery of grace - only that it meets us where we are but does not leave us where it found us. --Anne Lamott

Grace matters. For many, many reasons grace matters.

First, grace matters because it's God's idea. His idea of grace rebels against the "vulture culture" where society relishes in seeing people get what they deserve. God doesn't believe in "dog eat dog," "too little too late" or "only the strong survive." Grace matters because all of us, if we are honest with ourselves, need it. We've tried to fix others and ourselves with products, ideas and strategies. And yet, even with entire industries devoted to our internal and external improvement, it hasn't eliminated brokenness from our lives. We are still a planet of people in need of something better.

Grace matters because it changes things for the better. When grace is involved, even small actions can work toward repairing brokenness. "A tiny symbol of grace in the middle of the historic explosive conflict" can manage to disarm enemies.

And finally, grace matters because it is the trait at the very core of God's nature and the very reason why he sent Jesus. In Ephesians 2:7 it says God wants to "shower grace and kindness upon us in Jesus".

OPENING UP

1. If you are a new group, take a few minutes to introduce yourselves and get to know one another. Give a few insights on who you are and the things you are interested in. Keep it simple and brief. Share about your career, hobbies or favorite things to do.

If everyone already knows each other, feel free to skip this question.

2. What are some areas in our society where you fail to see grace or second chances extended? Can you think of a recent incident?

3. What do you hope to get out of this study?

PLAY SESSION ONE ON THE DVD NOW.

NOTES

GRACE MATTERS

DISCUSSION

1. Mike defined grace as "giving favor when it is undeserved." How would you describe grace?

2. In the video, the concept of radical honesty and saying whatever you think is mentioned. How transparent and honest should we be with people? What is the difference between "authentic harshness" and speaking the truth in love?

3. Do you think Christians or the church in general are good at giving second chances? Why or why not?

4. In what areas of your life (family, work, friends) could you show more grace? Are there certain people you tend to judge unfairly or more harshly?

STUDY

READ ACTS 15:36-41

Paul's passion and calling was to save those who were far from God. It was his mission. Barnabus was known as helping the underdog and being an encourager.

Earlier, Barnabus had come to Paul's defense when others were skeptical of this Christian killer's initial conversion. Now

Barnabus wanted to give this same kind of second chance to his nephew, John Mark. But Paul wasn't having it.

According to these verses, Paul thought going on a trip with John Mark was a bad idea because John Mark had deserted him on a previous trip. That meant Paul and Barnabus ended up on opposite sides of whether John Mark deserved a second chance.

Neither of the men would yield so Paul took off and left it up to Barnabus to give John Mark a second chance.

1. So who do you think was right? Paul or Barnabus? Do both have a legitimate argument?

2. Are you surprised by Paul's reaction knowing that earlier in his life he had been given a radical second chance? Should the second chances we've received impact giving second chances?

3. 2 Timothy 4:11 shows that Paul would eventually reconcile with John Mark. Paul, at the end of his life and while he was enduring deep suffering, specifically requests John Mark to come to him. What do you think this says about grace?

4. When you think about your willingness to give second chances? Are you more like Barnabus or Paul?

24 GRACENOMICS

ACTION & INSIGHT

An important component of growth is taking the thoughts, ideas and what we have learned in the Gracenomics group and turning them into credible actions. Here are a few action steps for the coming week.

1. Take some time this week and reflect on your beliefs about grace and second chances. Write out what grace means to you. It may help to brainstorm a list of characteristics you'd expect to see in someone who is living out the concepts in Gracenomics.

2. Write down a broken relationship or a situation that you would love to see improve over the next few weeks as you go through this study. Make it your project where the new strategy is grace.

3. This week identify an individual at your work, church or in your family. Choose to stand in their corner even though others are doubtful.

SESSION TWO:
GRACENOMICS FOR YOU

SUMMARY

Grace is knowing that there is nothing you can do to make God love you more. And there is nothing you could ever do that would make God love you less. -- Robert Brow

You're blessed when you're content with just who you are—no more, no less. --Matthew 5:5

We don't need to be reminded of our failures. They follow us like a shadow. We work hard to lose that shadow when we are with others, yet when we are alone we won't let it go. Somewhere within our inner reality we have a critical voice that calls out everything we are ashamed of. And all too often, we let that self-talk drain grace out of our lives every single day without doing anything about it.

Self-grace is a critically important component of living out *Gracenomics.* But for many people, this is sometimes one of the hardest areas to give grace. But just for a moment, imagine letting yourself "off the hook" and letting grace flow into the hurt, disappointment and screw-ups you've been hiding.

Gracenomics invites us into a place where we can let our failures be redeemed and used for good. Our past doesn't have to haunt us anymore. We can stop censoring our pasts; we no longer have to hide the things we feel embarrassed or ashamed of. We can make a choice to be free if we want to be.

OPENING UP

1. Do you think the world is obsessed with perfection? What are some examples that you see in the world today?

2. If you could be someone else, who would that someone else be? Why?

PLAY SESSION TWO ON THE DVD NOW.

NOTES

DISCUSSION

1. Mike mentions that our mistakes can define us, destroy us or strengthen us. In your life, which response is your default?

2. When we fail to invite grace into our failures or mistakes, what are some of the negative or unhealthy results?

3. In what areas of your life do you tend to be most critical about your performance? What have you been "scrubbing with a wire brush?"

4. Mike mentioned that when we honestly share our struggles and don't censor our story, we become a safe place for others to share their struggle. Do you agree?

STUDY

READ JOHN 18:1-11 AND 25-26

Peter, one of Jesus' best friends, had a lot to chew on. He had really messed up.

First, in the garden of Gethsemane, Peter committed an act of violence right in front of Jesus. Then selfishly looking out for his own interest, Peter denied that he even knew Jesus three times.

But even after all of this occurred, Jesus still used Peter in a powerful way.

However, Peter had to make a choice to either wallow in his failures or allow grace to have its way in his life. He held to the truth that even in his mistakes, Jesus would use him to build his church. Peter welcomed grace to come and restore his life.

Peter would never forget that night in Gethsemane but he did not let these moments define or destroy him.

1. Do you think it is possible that Peter's failures made him more effective for God? Explain.

2. Imagine you were labeled as the guy who almost murdered a man in front of Jesus and then later denied Christ three times. How would you move beyond these unfortunate labels and incidents?

GRACENOMICS

ACTION & INSIGHT

An important component of growth is taking the thoughts, ideas and what we have learned in the Gracenomics group and turning them into credible actions. Here are a few action steps for the coming week.

1. Write down the things in your past that you need to truly invite grace to heal. What events have you been "scrubbing with a wire brush" and need to let God forgive?

2. When you are out with friends this week, practice sharing both your successes and struggles. Both are important and relevant.

3. When you feel self-condemning thoughts creeping into your mind, ask God to take every negative thought captive. Stop. Pray. And embrace Gracenomics for yourself.

SESSION THREE:
GRACENOMICS FOR OTHERS

SUMMARY

God appoints our graces to be nurses to other men's weaknesses. --Henry Ward Beecher

It's not my ability, but my response to God's ability. That's what truly counts. --Corrie Ten Boon

You're blessed when you care. At the moment of being 'care-full,' you find yourselves cared for. --Matthew 5:7

Certain events in the world expose a rising hostility emerging in our relationships. News shows demonize politicians, religious leaders condemn other faiths and our freeways are filled with middle fingers and honking horns. The very bad news is that it seems like our ability to extend grace to each other is diminishing.

As a society, we find it very easy to be harsh about each other's mistakes. Reality TV thrives because we are entertained by people yelling and screaming at each other. Gossip magazines sell out because we love juicy celebrity scandals. And pubic officials win our votes by shoveling dirt on each other by the dump truck full. We love revenge and paybacks.

Often our judgment of others comes from our own weakness, impaired vision and skewed understanding. True grace is the exchange judgment for empathy. True *Gracenomics* is when you offer the same humanity to others that you use to filter your own life.

OPENING UP

1. Why do you think society loves to talk about celebrities or super star athletes that have failed?

2. When was the last time you got into an argument with someone? What was it about? Did it end well?

PLAY SESSION THREE ON THE DVD NOW.

NOTES

GRACENOMICS FOR OTHERS

DISCUSSION

1. List some specific examples where Christians feel justified withholding grace and forgiveness.

2. Who do you find it hard to give grace to? Is there a specific type of individual that drives you nuts?

3. Mike mentions that giving grace involves taking a risk and moving out of our comfort zones. Is it possible to give real grace without risking something?

4. Are you a person that is fast to forgive people or do you hold onto grudges? How does this impact you?

STUDY

READ LUKE 23:29-43

At the time of Jesus' crucifixion it was very important to promise to remember loved ones after their death. However, during Roman rule criminals were not usually shown this honor.

Their only epitaphs were their crimes, written and attached to the top of their crosses. These indictments became the last thing said of them, the thing for which they would be remembered. Similarly, criminals were not even afforded the basic right to burial. They had so little value in the eyes of society that their bodies were often thrown in a rubbish heap where the crows would feast on their corpses.

In the horror of his own crucifixion, Jesus offered a guilty man a special moment of grace: an epitaph that, despite his wrongdoing, could still read "worthy". In other words, Jesus' willingness to extend second chances extended even beyond death!

1. In light of this, what would Jesus' words "I will remember you" have meant for the criminal in his dying moments?

2. Without grace, what would the sign above your crucifixion cross say? What signs have you written above the cross of others?

44 GRACENOMICS

ACTION & INSIGHT

An important component of growth is taking the thoughts, ideas and what we have learned in the Gracenomics group and turning them into credible actions. Here are a few action steps for the coming week.

1. Make an honest list of any warped philosophies, barriers against truth, or bad theology that you are noticing you've come to believe about grace. Ask God to give you a new heart of grace for others.

2. Think of a friend who needs help rewriting the condemning epitaph above his or her cross. Call them. Encourage them. Tell them you care.

3. Who do you need to forgive? Be honest with this question. Are you unable or unwilling to give grace?

SESSION FOUR:
GRACENOMICS AT WORK

SUMMARY

The deepest principle in human nature is the craving to be appreciated. --William James

You're blessed when you can show people how to cooperate instead of compete or fight. That's when you discover who you really are, and your place in God's family. --Matthew 5:9

Gracenomics has serious pay off in the business world as well. At work, grace becomes an umbrella term that covers a whole family of behaviors – everything from being tactful to responding responsibly to conflict and even to listening well. Exercising this sort of grace stirs goodwill in clients and employees, even if they don't formally identify our acts as grace.

But *Gracenomics* is about more than spreading warm fuzzies to clients. Grace actually affects the bottom line. It has muscles and teeth. Grace breeds long term customer relationships and referral business because clients and employees trust your company has their best interests at heart and believe you work hard to understand their perspectives when problems arise.

The desire to belong to a group—even if it is a group of loyal customers--is part of our human nature. Sadly, group identity is often abused rather than celebrated. When two groups come into contact, it is often their differences that are emphasized. Because of this, group identity is also often used as an excuse for conflict, or to hide other issues.

OPENING UP

1. Describe your first job. Did you enjoy it or was it a bad experience?

2. Do you think grace should be a critical part of the work culture? Why or why not?

PLAY SESSION FOUR ON THE DVD NOW.

NOTES

GRACENOMICS AT WORK

DISCUSSION

1. How can you practically help others win in what they are doing?

2. Mike talked about how listening is a key component of *Gracenomics*. Rate your listening skills on a scale of 1-10. Share your number with the group and explain why you gave yourself this score.

3. *Gracenomics* is important when pursuing our dreams or launching new initiatives. Why do you think the fear of failure or criticism is so powerful?

4. Dietrich Bonhoffer connects our ability to listen to each other with the real ability to listen to God. Do you think this true?

5. "Ubuntu" is an African philosophy of not being threatened by each other. Why do you think we are often jealous of others successes or threatened by others skills?

STUDY

READ 1 CORINTHIANS 12:12-26

In this passage, Paul lays out an important metaphor. He compares those who believe to parts of the human body. Each person and each part serves a different purpose, but—he reminds—all these purposes contribute to the whole.

Paul had to come up with this metaphor because some Christians in Corinth thought they were better than others. They believed their gifts were more important and valuable. And as a result, other Christians in Corinth thought they had no gifts at all. This naturally lead to jealousy between the supposedly "non-gifted" and "importantly gifted".

To set them straight, Paul stressed that the parts of the body are connected. If one part suffers the other parts suffer too. If something good happens in the body everyone benefits. No part can work on its own. When Christians are truly acting the way God intended, they respect each other and celebrate together.

1. What gifts do you see elevated within our society? In the church? How can we work for equality and unity?

2. Many in Corinth felt they had no gifts to offer or that their skills were not important? Do you ever think this about your own gifts?

ACTION & INSIGHT

An important component of growth is taking the thoughts, ideas and what we have learned in the Gracenomics group and turning them into credible actions. Here are a few action steps for the coming week.

1. Reflect on the things that come natural for you or that you consider a unique gift from God. Write down these skills or gifts. How could you use them to help others?

2. Experiment this week by turning your phone off at all meals or meetings. In your conversations fight the urge to be distracted. Practice being fully present to value the people around you.

3. Write a note to a friend or co-worker celebrating their gifts and expressing how thankful you are for their contributions to the world.

ABOUT PEOPLE OF
THE SECOND CHANCE

You're blessed when you get your inside world—your mind and heart—put right. Then you can see God in the outside world.--Matthew 5:8

People of the Second Chance is a global movement of individuals dedicated to transforming lives through radical grace and second chances. Established in October, 2010, this innovative non-profit focuses on four key areas:

1. CREATE SECOND CHANCE ADVOCATES & FACILITATE ACTION ORIENTED COMMUNITY

2. PRODUCE SECOND CHANCE TOOLS AND RESOURCES

3. ELEVATE AND LEGITIMIZE NEW CONVERSATIONS ABOUT GRACE IN THE PUBLIC FORUM

4. PROVIDE STRATEGIC AND SPIRITUAL COUNSEL FOR INDIVIDUALS IN CRISIS OR COMEBACKS

For more information on People of the Second Chance visit www.POTSC.com

CONTACT INFORMATION

CONTACT MIKE:
Mike@POTSC.com

CONTACT PEOPLE OF THE SECOND CHANCE:
Contact@POTSC.com

STORE:
www.POTSC.com/store

SPEAKING INQUIRIES:
Kristen@POTSC.com

QUESTIONS AND FEEDBACK:
Contact@POTSC.com

WEBSITE:
www.POTSC.com

NEXT STEPS

ONLINE
Join the dynamic community of second chancers at www.POTSC.com. You can also connect with us on the following social networks at www.Facebook.com/POTSC or on Twitter @POTSC or @MikeFoster

MOBILE
Download our FREE People of the Second Chance Iphone app through Itunes to keep up to date with new blog posts, photos and videos.

JOIN THE MOVEMENT
Visit the People of the Second Chance website at www.POTSC.com to join the movement of radical grace and second chances.

GRACE MOB
The Grace Mob is a highly committed team of passionate individuals who are combating judgment with tangible acts of grace and love.

SPEAKING
Mike Foster is available to present on the core issues of GRACENOMICS and how to unleash second chance living. If you are interested in hosting a Second Chance Sunday please email Kristen@POTSC.com